INLANDIA

INLANDIA

K A NELSON

RECENT
WORK
PRESS

Inlandia
Recent Work Press
Canberra, Australia

ISBN: 9780648257905 (paperback)

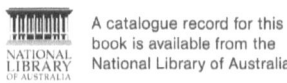

NATIONAL LIBRARY OF AUSTRALIA
A catalogue record for this book is available from the National Library of Australia

Cover illustration: Billie's Garden Landscape (detail), 1989,
screenprint on tea towel,
© Jan Mackay.
Cover photograph: David Paterson, Dorian Photographics
Cover design by Recent Work Press

Set by Silvana Moro

recentworkpress.com

For Noni
In memory of Ethel Jean Nelson (nee Sibley) 1927-2016

Contents

Come to where I've been ...

... where I'm from

... where I am

Come to where I've been ...

To Lajamanu, 1981

Discarded beer cans—sun-bleached-flat-white—
pockmark deep graded gutters; frayed arcs of dull rubber
pitched from road trains in heat, curl
around saplings/spinifex/termite mounds;
car bodies lie where engines died.

In cattle country now. The stench of road kill
fills the cabin; crows scatter and resettle on swollen/split
carcasses. I accelerate.

At Top Springs roadhouse, whitefellas
prop up the bar. Variegated ankles spill out
unlaced sandshoes/low-slung Stubbies
show aging cracks/dimpled buttocks.

One old bloke stinks of stale piss—looks harmless enough—
cups his hand/whispers, *G'day darlin', wanna fuck?*
Another grins, toothless, the rest snigger/laugh.

I hold my tongue/think: the blackfellas
at Lajamanu have to be a breath of fresh air.

Culture shock

God?
There isn't one.
The Dreaming is a blur.
Anthropologists? No help at all.

I've become
cellmate
to a reptile.
In his terrarium
I climb walls of glass, slide back, slide back, back slide ...

I eat insects tweezered in. Professor Jeckle teases me—
bends over my cage, lets down his beard like Rapunzel in drag
jerks back
when I reach up ...

I'm not permitted, I'm not allowed. I can't see through.
Thinking is skewed. Navigation impaired

Warlpiri maps
Greek to me—
make nonsense of my compass

in my second childhood
taking baby steps
my nappy chafes and
there's no mother to change me

*

in this
circus tent
i have no tricks
or fancy dress the one
trapeze hangs by a thread and
besides i have no head for widths

i cannot sleep

outside
dim stars
sweat ...
the milky way seems to be the only road map out of here
but i can't read it ...

Broken promise drive

(Alice Springs, Christmas, 1983—
developers blew up a sacred site so
work on Barrett Drive could progress
to the nearby casino)

It takes a man to set a trap

It takes a man to tell a lie

It takes a man to lay a charge

It takes a man to light a fuse

It takes a man to turn away

It takes a man to half explain

It takes a hundred men, they wail,

to move a caterpillar's tail

It takes another man or four

to mop a dirty courthouse floor

with forty-thousand years of lore.

Women's business

The first time
I saw Napangardi
she was walking
barefoot
along a track
from Top Camp
towards the Council building
dressed in a white uniform.
A red scarf
flattened the grey hair
against her head.
Stitched on her breast
pocket in blue script,
Women's Brigade.
When I greeted her
she said, *Name Ruby.*
I clean this place.

And she did.

The last time
I saw Napangardi
she was organising
a ceremony in a sacred
place for women.
Dressed in a red skirt
her grey hair,
loose and wild,
budgerigar feathers
caught in curls.
When she pointed
her digging stick
and began
the white clay
on her breasts
seemed to pour
into the rising dust.
She said, *Do like this, Nangala.*

And I did.

Two worlds

Bureaucrats board a plane bound for Arnhem Land
briefcasebrains brimming with *balanda* bus-i-ness
    looking down on rivers snaking their way to the Arafura Sea
    remember prayers that come to mind in times of stress

Our Father, who art in heaven, hallowed be thy name ...

Touching down, they breathe in relief—it smells of salt, smoke, sweat
a tricky mimih spirit leaps and disappears into lungs, bloodstream, bones
    they move in landcruisers to air-conditioned buildings
    check for missed calls or messages on their latest mobile phones

For what we are about to receive, Lord make us truly thankful ...

Inside, the empty whiteboard shines, the coloured markers wait
water bubbles in the urn, the upturned mugs—stained—but clean
    the mob lean on walls, squat or straddle chairs
    bureaucrats sit up the front, a united bureaucratic team

I wish to pay my respects to the traditional custodians of this land ...

While protocols are trotted out inside, the women sit cross-legged
in the shade, pick at scabs—old wounds still hurt—
    talk, laugh, look beyond the tarmac and the trees
    camp dogs stretch, kids with sticks draw circles in the dirt

Yawkyawks float on their backs in the greenblue bay ...

Whitefella residents know the ropes, they're first to voice their deep concerns
talk up strong in acronyms, refer to notes, know all the ways
    to keep their vested interests alive, close to their clammy chests
    they work all the working week, mow imported lawns on Sundays

Wangara stirs the leaves, disturbs the trees ...

Meanwhile, elders toss ideas around—how to live in two worlds
grow up kids right way, no more gunja, no more grog. That future in their heads
    they talk up learning English, teaching the Rom and Mandayin
    plans are made to hatch like turtle eggs in nearby sheds

Old bones in hollow logs applaud, knowing how to wait ...

Katherine, 1981

My vision of hell—
The back bar of a Katherine hotel,
Friday night.

Ringers from nearby
stations front the bar,
stay well past closing time.

Women off country
slap brown arms around men
in exchange for booze.

In Katherine
shopkeepers stare, spit, whisper,
make snide remarks

as Jakamarra,
Warlpiri elder, walks
beside me

his felt hat tipped forward
hiding his handsome face.
Unlike my husband

he's tee-total—
wouldn't be seen dead
in a Katherine hotel.

Palm Island kids

Don't walk through that yard, miss.
See the Hairyman?
See him!

There! There, in the window?
That black one.
He's a real tall skinny one.
He's a real strong one, too.

What's your name, miss?

I got a sister called that, too.

She's only seben.

See how the Hairyman looks dead now
but he's real at night.
The Hairyman's a scary man
who can blink.

See his yellow eyes?

He'll blink at you if you go in there.

He'll *grab* you if you go in there.

He'll ***eat*** you if you go in there.

You got any kids, miss?

Lookout! The Hairyman's blinking now!
See! See, his eyes moving?
Stay here, on the road
with us.
Come this way.

Where you from, miss?

You got any lollies?

That old man's story

We sit outside, discuss the day...
Old Charlie reminds me of Uncle Ray—
always on about the youth of today:

> Sun come on up, sun e go down
> Got no money to work all o that ground
> An my people keep askin me when, when, when?
>
> We sit down on country, now we old men
> Speak up real strong, strong for our land
> Sun come on up, sun e go down.
>
> We got all o our stories, our dance an our song
> Got plenty o water, bores all along
> An my people keep askin me, when, when, when?
>
> When we was young men, we'd come an we'd go
> We'd come an we'd go with cattle, go drovin
> Sun come on up, sun e go down.
>
> Some sit down nothin, they drink an play card
> Talk up the Dreamin, lie on swags in the yard
> An my people keep askin me, when, when, when?
>
> Countrymen done it, can do it again
> Young men should stand up, use muscle an brain
> An my people stop askin me, when, when, when?

'What about Elias, Bevan, Bessie and Fay—
young people who work hard for their pay?'
Old Charlie punches his palm, 'Not like in my day!'

Dead end narrative (triptych)

(Three responses to Cait Wait's painting, 'First Time Inside, 1998-2014')

1
The road to town is a road to crime—
Stay here boy, learn your lore
His father's words, another time

The road was straight, it looked sublime
He travelled fast, flew like the crow
The road to town is a road to crime

He looked around, the view was fine
A father, tribe, a law outgrown
His father's words, another time

He stayed in town, he crossed a line
The tavern's bar was quite a show
The road to town is a road to crime

There was no reason, or any rhyme
He couldn't recall the fatal blow
His father's words, another time

A distant echo in his mind
Now the boy is locked inside
The road to town is a road to crime
His father's words, another time

2

There's a songline he was born to sing
Stories pre-ordained he had to tell
A dance to dance, a tribe and all his kin
And yet we find him here inside this cell

Shades, black and faceless, hover close to him
Deep shadows hold despite the time of day
His homeland memories grow thin
Thoughts of kin, a new dismay

His song is murder every night relived
The tempo of his dance is deathly slow
His story is a dead end narrative
Of what he'll never do and never know

Two laws broken, a life entombed
country's dying, one songline ruined

3

hard labour
good behaviour
did is time fer murder

songline mendin
nothin's endin
e's painted up fer ceremony

This is a woman

(Response to Cait Wait's painting, 'Mrs Abbott', 2006;
also refers to many senior Aboriginal women)

In the early hours of these bitter mornings
when the fog comes down and settles;
when the only cars on Commonwealth Avenue
are taxis changing shifts or ministerial staff cars
taking lackeys home; when flags hang slack
in the dark, stiffen in the cold on their steel poles;
my thoughts fly north to the desert—to a woman
who calls me daughter, who took me to Dinner Camp
told me a story, taught me a song, showed me a dance:

This is a woman who travels the land
Where stories are danced and country is sung
Where magic and myth is retold in the sand
Where kinship and totems are like lines on a hand

This is a woman who travels with women
Whose customs and life move in time with the moon
Whose birth on a songline means obligation
Whose night sky is peopled with ancestral kin

This is a woman who travels with crows
Who glides across country as hunter and healer
Who teaches clanswomen all that she knows
Who carries the lore wherever she goes

This is a woman who travels around
on everywhere roads criss-crossing the land
Knows bitumen highways lead to trouble in town
gridlock the cities, spoil old hunting grounds

In the early hours my thoughts fly north to the desert—
to a woman I call mother, who took me to Dinner Camp
told me a story, taught me a song, showed me a dance.

She is a woman now elder and leader
She is a woman who travels the land
She is a woman who longs for old times
She is a woman, the last of her kind.

Machinery of the 98%

An imaginary

One time, Wally Jampijinpa, Nora Napangarti and all that mob,
left the humbug of the station and the settlement behind
to live on their *estate* just inside the border near a soak that runs
all year long. They were happy, though some might call it
living rough. They spent their days growing up the kids
strong in law and chasing game. They pooled welfare
cheques to keep the *Troopie* running smooth.

Meanwhile, down south, Minister Brough (it rhymes with *rough*)
devised a clever plan of action with a departmental mate
nicknamed *Crash*, (short for *crash-or-crash-through*) to change
the fate of Wally, Nora and the mob using the *Little Children
are Sacred* report as the ruse—a tactic favoured by ex-army
personnel, like Mal.

The secret plan had Honest John walking briskly round the lake.
His well-honed snout sniffed the wind of one more easy win.
With this in mind, the PM rubber-stamped Mal's cunning plan;
Crash waited in the wings to implement it, quicktime,
with assistance from his obedient, expert public service staff.

Sometimes Wal and Nora took their turn with old Gyprock
and his daughter, Nell, to work the dots on canvas with a stick.
Their acrylic stories graced the walls and floors of galleries
in Alice Springs. With the extra cash, the mob bought fresh
supplies and hurried home, out of that troubled town.

This mob knew their dreaming. They married right skin way,
mostly. Despite *tjuringas* going west and east and north,
but nearly always south, they knew their country and its
ceremonies. They kept and taught the lore in song and dance

as best they could, in spite of the slow breaking down
of nearly everything.

Moving right along (not '*Moving Forward*' yet), the mandarin's request was clear. All departmental staff should be seated in the theatrette at Tuggeranong by noon or in a room where the presentation could be beamed to all thirty odd branch offices around the continent. It was: *The most important breaking policy in thirty years of Indigenous public administration.* Or so the email said.

* * *

One shaft of light fell through the open double doors into the auditorium. Staff filed in, eyes adjusting to the dark. Seats taken, small talk buzzed—current projects, kids' school marks, travel, the frequent flyer points clocked up that month—then the spotlight and a moment's silence.

Stage right a door swings wide. Six or seven suited bureaucrats in ties or scarves, a hint of gold on fingers, wrists and lobes, take their places on the podium; the mandarin steps up behind the lectern, taps the mic; audio and camera roll without a hitch.

The mandarin begins as most in charge still do, with acknowledgement of country, some pleasantries and thank yous. He motions to the legal team, *please stand*, asks the audience (or is that *commands*?) to show their appreciation for the expertise and dedication, but most of all, the responsiveness, to Minister Brough. This new legislation, devised in tripletime (overtime penalty rates implied) required dexterity to obviate impediments in existing laws, not to mention the midnight oil burnt for those in charge of marbled halls in that Great House lying slightly north, as the crow flies.

Each bureaucrat named, stands proud, tired, satisfied with a job well done. Relaxed and comfortable, someone cracks a little joke about public service medals down the track. Applause dies down. The mandarin inquires of the crowd if there are questions for the noble group.

Seconds tick by, one to five. At least one heart in the auditorium beats double time, remembers Wally, Nora and the mob, still blithely unaware of this new law and what it will mean for them. *Six, seven, eight, nine.* One hand goes up, a lass stands, speaks without benefit of microphone, testosterone.

You say the intervention or 'emergency response' will have its phases,
that down the track you plan to build my people's capacity. Please sir, tell us
more about that phase, sir, tell us who and what and when will that take place?
And the mandarin (he promised zero tolerance for workplace bullying on taking up the job) defers to *Crash*, after all, he is Mal's man.

A beady eye or two fixes on the miscreant, *Crash* does what most bullies, do well. He *condemns*. He condemns black corporations, homelands and settlements as *museums*, gives black parents their fair share of condemnation, to justify the first two phases: Intervention 1 and Intervention 2. Building capacity? Ignored. He ducks and weaves with legal-ease, talks up his vision aligning *ex-act-ly* with the Minister's, reminds us, for good measure, of what all good public servants are paid to do.

Most left that day dazzled by the plan's audacity. A few left saddened by the power-brokers' self-congratulation. Others thought of little kids (their blighted innocence). Some pondered the politics of race those in power use to keep themselves in that power-place. The questioning lass wondered if the 2% had any chance at all when the machinery of the 98% rolled on further north.

⋆ ⋆ ⋆

The government changed, not so the policies. Bureaucrats moved on, some to higher paying jobs. Those for and those against the intervention grow in numbers. The left are at each other's throats. Stronger Futures morphed into a strategy with the word *advancement* in the mix. Brough and Crash have sunk from view.

Wally's on the grog, Nora's down, not out, living in a Growth Town with the kids in tow. She's painting less but sometimes sells her Dreaming in the mall with Nell. They get letters from the feds—turn up for meetings on such and such a day and time or else you'll be cut off. The kids eat take-away for breakfast but they are in school, forgetting other lessons.

Out at the soak, the broken windmill tilts. It seems a bone's been pointed at the country or its been sung by some deep southern magic. Wally took old Gyprock's passing badly. The family pooled their cash to bury him out bush with due respect. As the mound of earth above his coffin settles, plastic flowers fade to white.

Chorus of crows

When she saw Top Camp
(humpies made of corrugated iron/slabs of bark
people and dogs living together
children discharge running from nostrils/ears
like sewage seeping from the broken pipes next door)
she didn't wince.
She learnt to overlook the rubbish
caught on broken fences
blown by westerlies that brought the dust
and the haunting sound of crows through
every crack.

When she met Topsy
(her husband used a star picket
punished her tribal way even though everyone knew
that whitefella contractor got the better of her)
she didn't faint.
It wasn't the first time she'd seen human flesh
open to the bone or held the hand of a woman
being stitched up.
Outside the clinic the crows seemed to sing
that white man
long gone.

When the Land Council mob
said no to a drink in the back bar
(the publican would only lace
their beer with Worcestershire Sauce
customers would stare/whisper behind cupped hands)
she bought a carton.
They sat in the yard yarning and laughing

at the crows as they burnt their beaks
scavenging for scraps
on the barbecue
hot plate.

When she walked across the Harbour Bridge
arm in arm with friends
(*black/white/brindle*
as her Nana used to say)
mothers pushed babies in strollers
fathers shouldered children waving flags
people carried placards
and a breeze billowed out
that 'sorry' word above the crowd for hours.
Not a crow in sight!

Well into the New Millenium
it wasn't the daily press releases
of suicides/sniffing/stoushes
or claims the ATSIC experiment
had failed (miserably)
but another order from a minister
and a mandarin
carried out by men in overalls
that did her in.

When they took the dotted/cross-hatched worlds
    off all the office walls to hoard them
in a secret storeroom somewhere
    (Mitchell/Fyshwick/Tuggeranong?)
when each piece of art and artifact was placed
    (without bubble wrap or due regard)
in Woolworths shopping trolleys

that lurched along the corridor
their wobbly wheels protesting to the last
when workers sat transfixed to telephones
and screens (like crows on a carcass pecking
pecking, unperturbed by passing cars)
she hurried to the women's toilet
locked the door/flushed
and wept.

Later she stared at her blank wall
where Rover's *Universe* used to hang.
Without him she felt so far removed
from Top Camp
Topsy and the mob
from the fly speck she said she was
in a far flung corner of his print
near one of five gold dots
(or sacred sites)
and as she stared
she thought she heard him say
gardiya might like 'em
might learn 'em
might read 'em right way
one day.

But beyond the blank space/concrete wall/double glass
it seemed to her the crows guffawed
(as if they foresaw
the NT Intervention).

The long view

If I were home in Canberra today, I'd be sitting in my local
café sipping lattes, reading the weekend papers. Instead,
I'm living in the desert: four hours from a decent coffee
or weekend news; two from a roadhouse where a dodgy bar
and greasy spoon co-exist, like I do here, quite comfortably,
despite two laws in play, a different lingo, multiple requests
from locals to help translate demanding and persistent letters
from our government or a certain company chasing overdue
instalments or compound interest on hired white goods
long since broken. Meanwhile, the herbal tea is cooling,
breakfast's over, the watered garden's looking pert.
What I love to do on Saturdays and Sundays is take in
the long view south through slim venetians that slice
the desert landscape horizontally. If I look west I see
nasturtiums curling closer to the closed glass doors,
their blooms, like miniature suns, are kinder than the one
above. The peewee will arrive mid morning to make
the same old love to his image in the side mirror of my 4 x 4
parked outside in semi shade. I'll clean his mess off later,
when it's cool. Right now this weekend idyll is shattered
by the sound of donkeys rutting in the run-down shelter
of a nearby donga; the poetry of camp dogs barking
in the distance; the roar of a mob at war outside the store ...
They're in a sweat, sorting out a recent problem or some
age-old gripe still unresolved and festering. It seems to me
the crows assembled on the sagging fence line near the school
egg them on. Obscenities in a desert tongue drift to my place.
The poor nasturtiums seem to cringe. Some whitefellas here say
the reasons for the fighting are long forgotten, people fight
for love of fighting. That's not my view. Decisions over land
some decades past; how last week's royalties were divvied up;
the local power brokers' influence on town committees and
the affluence of that family plays a part. Though trouble-

makers do love trouble. It's really much the same where I come from. Some people, no matter where they live, like to pour accelerant on flames and watch things burn. This might not be home to me but a familiar sounding siren reminds me of home. The cops will impound improvised weapons, lock someone up, negotiate a simmering peace, which may or may not prevail.

As the temperature climbs to 48 degrees, I'll turn the air-con up to high, put a CD on, look towards that long view south, without any hankering for my distant city home.

Induction (intercultural field)

(Apologies to Craig Storti, 'The Art of Crossing Cultures', 1989)

Don't go overseas to feel at home. Remember what Lord Byron said: *travel makes us feel as if we exist.* You came for difference, adventure, risk, experience, or should have, *Expatriate*! Don't think of *them* as 'foreign'.

The bunker mentality is a little death. Taking refuge in the foreign *colony's* sub-culture, that exclusive Club—its gin & tonic set—is a python that will squeeze out every breath. And don't become a cultural malcontent if disappointment makes its presence felt.

Those who seem like strangers might be your own kind: thirsty mono-cultural drinkers, faultfinders, who need superiority in every sip. Blunder on, even though you may be affronted or cause effrontery ... be *all thumbs*, just have a go at cracking codes, walking in mismatched, ill-fitting shoes, or bare feet.

The joke's on you so laugh a lot and at yourself. Be content with your cultural identikit. You'll need your fellow countrymen and women, books and music, meat and three veg—any well-worn reality check—for balance and perspective.

Sometimes.

Make sure you leave a trail of crumbs or stones you can follow home. Learn to go without, make do. To *function* is a virtue, like learning. Don't expect to triumph as you map new country. Learn its legends and its rules, its longitudes and latitudes. Lifelines, safety nets, inflated tyre tubes might include: a good night's sleep, a daily dose of barley greens, writing letters home or skype-ing if you have the internet.

Stay well clear of zealots, those who love the un-holy dollar (or its local equivalent) and misogynists. Eat well. Learn the lingo—it is, by far, the best way to understanding everything. Adjust, but not too much. Sometimes the greatest compliment is not to budge on right or wrong. As for *going native*, don't be that kind of *schmuck*. A full transition is impossible and not your mission—it is nearly always viewed with suspicion by compatriots and hosts alike. It's best to meet half way, your other half.

A snippet of history

I was born on Wiradjiri land but didn't know that growing up.
At school we learnt convict settlement, governors,
wheat, wool, gold, English kings and queens.

The Wiradjiri? Nowhere to be seen.

Windradyne, that hard campaigner in the frontier wars,
is a footnote in one settler family's history. He spared them
when other settler families were slain that day.

Why was that family spared, allowed to stay?

One young man in the family learnt the language.
On that bloody day, he spoke to Windradyne with ease,
as his equal in that unequal war.

Battles, skirmishes, martial law declared.

Windradyne, also known as 'Saturday', walked to Sydney
in a top hat, the English word 'PEACE' written
on a bit of cardboard, tucked in the ribbon band.

The governor was much relieved.

This I learnt when I was forty-three.

Another snippet of history

dillybag, coolamon
bark and river reed
fur and feathers
digging stick and seed
black crow and cockleshell
eel trap, echidna quill
shrimp scoop
possum skin
bora ring, bora ring
midden, midden, midden ...

boomerang, waddy, spear and shield
rifle, bullet, well-honed blade
union jack
alphabet
unmarked grave ...

Memento mori

For Helen

after the lawn sale
the rest of her things
are given away to clear
the house for the buyer
                                        seller/inheritor

the tjanpi basket comes my way
its rim decorated with wisps
of blue wool threaded
through once-red ininti beans

                                        brown/decaying

it holds six smooth patterned river rocks
that pleased the artist's palm, the artist's eye
and pleases mine; an almost oval piece of wood
blade-shaped, a dot painting

                                        bird/echidna

a torn and faded silk daffodil sits
beside a small piece of denim hemmed
on two sides, curled and frayed.
A simple two by two inch square

                                        old measurements/older memories

cut and twinned with the daffodil. Yellow leopard
skin pattern—crutch of my old jeans—
memento of our long week end, the way
they unpeeled in her double swag

under stars/moon

a five cent piece, purple paper clip
silver staple, a bent and rusty nail, dust
confirms how the meaning of gifts can unravel—
how love itself moves between

keepsake/relic

I wash the river rocks until they sing
polish the dotted bird/echidna
bin the daffodil and denim
put aside till later the cast off

coin/metallica

Years ago, someone told me
tjanpi baskets decorated with wool
become fodder for moths. I know this
to be true as I remove the frail yarn with

fingernails/darning needle

I thread the eye with loud pink raffia.
Red beans, already hotwired, await a lifeline.
I begin the slow work of attachment
recall her last soft morphine drift ...

tjanpi basket/wooden casket

... where I'm from

Four poems from the Wallawa Road Suite

I Archie Boy

was always old.
Every morning, every evening
he unwound bandages on his lower legs,
dressed ulcers with thick ointment
from a tin with a screw-top lid.

He let me play 'horsey' on his legs,
'jig-a-jig-jig to Banbury Cross',
ride to Thistle Station and back again.

When he tired of that—I never did—he'd twist
my tongue with 'Peter Piper picked a pickled pepper'.

His working day was sheep—
    birthing lambs in spring,
    crutching, dipping, shearing,
    killing hoggets for homestead meat.
    When the woolclip hit the bank
    He'd buy the latest Holden

    —and sawing, splitting, mending fences,
    building woolsheds with his brother,
    my grandfather, clearing land
    for grazing or a crop.

He had a hand in milking, trapping rabbits,
shooting kangaroos or targets. He helped
neighbours. Like the Mitchells, he talked
weather, farming, fencing, land and family sagas.

He loved a riddle,
loved Great Aunt Elsie, Jeanie, Jim,
Jenny, their progeny
and me.

At our last goodbye, he lay foetal on a bed
in a west end nursing home. I pulled
a cotton blanket up to his stubbled chin,
kissed his wrinkled forehead, whispered,
Love you, Archie Boy to a deaf ear.

II 1950-1955 – Small points in time

Standing at their open doors they saw dust rise
behind slow-moving cars. They knew who
traversed that road, where they were going and what for ...

They knew every ringtone
on the party line and listened in.

Come dark, they lit their lamps. By day, they cleaned
the blackened glass, trimmed wicks, rubbed dust
from decorated parts and bowls with soft rags,

tenderly, as if every wish they made
would come to pass.

They felt the warmth of fire in a hearth, sat there early evenings
spoke of their working day, told tall stories. They kept the fire burning
in a backlog that could be rekindled in the morning.

They felt fire lash their land
and formed their own brigade.

Between each Sunday service, held nine miles away, they prayed
for rain or for the rain to cease. Five families. Five families bound
by land, one dirt road and common interests.

Bound by one God, three religions—Presbyterian,
Roman Catholic, Church of England—and one Eden.

Gardens! Vegetables, flowers, fruit trees blossomed. They killed
sheep and chickens for their tables, kept milking cows,
sold calves on.

Entrails went to working dogs,
scraps to chickens or to compost.

They sang their songs of praise in church or standing 'round a pianola
at *Glengarry*. Little kids, like me, could play it, if we could reach
the pedals. They sang along with perforated rolls

decoded lyrics outside their experience:
Carousel, The Skater's Waltz, The Student Prince.

In the Empire Hall a fiddler's repertoire catered for
their taste in music, their common love of dance. They would Strip
the Willow, choose new partners for the Pride of Erin or the waltz.

Their formula for joy: Pops on wooden dance floors, suppers made
by women of the CWA, Frank Bourke & the White Rose Orchestra.

Adult men took up children in their arms, taught them the rhythm
and the tempo of familial love, hinting what might come of that.
Women danced with other women when short of men,

who strolled outside to share a long neck
with a mate or take a leak beneath the Southern Cross.

This world is lost except to memory—mine, my brothers and our
cousins. The road remains unsealed, their farms sold on. In a nearby
cemetery, five families rest in separate coffins, separate graves,

in three denominations. Dates of birth and death
denote small points in time and nothing in between.

III Original inhabitants

The people we knew and loved lived two generations
removed from settler ancestors who took up land.

They retold tales their parents told of 'olden days',
did not recall an Aboriginal shepherd showing old man Kerr

a lump of gold. In the local library I looked at history books,
found Kerr had cut the hundredweight in half, transported it

by horse and dray to a town a hundred miles off to weigh
and value it. As small reward, Kerr gave the shepherd

a flock and bonds. This history reckoned the corroboree
went on and on 'till everything was gone. Another history

claims the shepherd's name was *Irvine*. Others don't mention
him by name or record an Aboriginal shepherd's part at all

in that glittering saga. I wonder where he came from?
One of these days, I'll take a Murray's bus to Sydney,

walk to the Mitchell Library, see if *Irvine* was *Wiradjiri*,
fossick in the mullock heap of our shared history.

IV Cracker night

Jimmy pulls old stumps, chains them to a tractor—
the one with iron wheels and cleats—drags them to a clearing,
leaving ruts so deep, only my head sticks out as I follow on behind.
(*That's how small I is!*)

Archie Boy hauls rotting fence posts in the Bedford.
His 'little helper', I keep an eye out for a rabbit, kangaroo, or fox.
He has a .22 behind the driver's seat, a box of bullets in the glove box.
(*'Don't touch the bullets or the gun'*, he says, *'til you turn twenty-one'*.)

Jean and Jenny gather rubbish from the garden in an old wheelbarrow,
wheel it down the track. I tag along, pick up dead gum leaves,
toss them on a heap. Jeanie says they burn like paper.
(*I like the smell.*)

Aunty Else cleans out the laundry. Old newspapers—
Mudgee Guardians—pile up behind the laundry door.
'Fire hazard', she declares, then sighs.
'Here, carry this, my Kittalee'.
(*That's her special name for me.*)

Tom Thumbs, Double Bungers
Roman Candles, Catherine Wheels,
Sparklers, Sky Rockets ...
bagged and boxed on a Friday shopping trip to town.

Everyone down Wallawa Road goes to town on Fridays.
They'll come to 'Glengarry' on cracker night,
to 'Merryangledre' next Sunday to play tennis
and, come September, we'll all help
Archie Boy at shearing time.
(*Jimmy puts me in the wool press.*)

Cracker night is Cracker Night in this neck of the woods.
(*I don't care who Guy Fawkes is.*)

Behind the counter

In my father's barber shop
I sold cigarettes and matches,
pouches of tobacco,
Tally-Ho

took money for haircuts
and gave out the proper change.
After every customer
I swept up

watched my father
hone a blade on leather,
make small talk with a farmer
brush hairy residue
off thick, red necks.

I restacked pipes in sweeping arcs,
displayed Brylcreem to advantage,
answered the black telephone.

Did I want to be the woman
blowing smoke rings
in that poster on the wall?

In lieu of wages
I stole cigarettes and chewing gum.
My favourite brands
were Juicy Fruit and Marlboro.

Sometimes I dressed the window.
As I wound crepe paper
round a cardboard cylinder
to make a barber's pole,
I made a vow: I would never
work behind a counter,
cut anybody's hair except my own.

My father said

children should be seen and not heard;
don't talk about sex, politics or religion;
think about the family name, my reputation;

be home by ten p.m. or else you'll never
get the car again; and see that razor strop
hanging on the laundry wall?

When my father put on the hat
of a philosopher, he said there were more
good people in the world than bad.

He rose above his troubles flying
single-engine aeroplanes,
came back to earth, drank too much.

Two sheets to the wind, my father sang
one song. Not *Danny Boy*. He preferred
a version of *Mother Machree* that went on

and on ... My father had one joke
about Siam he called a piece of shrapnel
from the war. His victim had to bend and rise

and bend again, recite these words: *Ah, what a goo!*
Ah, what a goo! It was a long, drawn out performance.
To end, the poor sod had to add, *Siam*.

One night, three sheets to the wind,
My father looked at me and said,
One day those big brown eyes will lead
you to your ruin. Then he made a beeline
for his bed, singing so off key (in this I take after him)
he could never be mistaken for an Irishman.

Sometimes there was a poem

In the corner of my parents' shed, the table slumps,
burdened with the things you find in sheds:

    a hammer and a drill, screws, nails
    of different lengths and widths in tins.

I don't want it sold, or taken to the rubbish tip,
but I can't take it home. I have the family silver,
the dinner set (my brothers have the guns)
and, besides, I'm cleaning out my own garage.

The table (rectangular, mission brown) seats six.
Instead of legs it has a fancy panel either end
with footrests we scrambled for as kids.

At weekday evening meals, Mum doled out stories
from her childhood, like dessert. Sometimes
there was a poem. Those nights, my father's meal
was covered with a plate, placed in a 'warming
drawer' beneath the new electric stove.

Home late, Dad ate alone, picked at his food—
too full of beer and talk with other men
like him, assembled in the Soldiers Club.

At breakfast time we came, reluctantly,
to the table one by one, to eat our porridge.

    One word out of place,
    one tired complaint,

and Dad would THUMP the table, instead of us.

Sundays, we sat together for lunch.
One of us said Grace, Dad carved the roast,
Mum sat down last. Afterwards, Dad went
to the aerodrome to fly a Tiger Moth. When Mum
and I washed up, sometimes there was a poem.

Early lessons

1

My father wrote the nine times table on the toilet wall in texta. He said, *That's where you wile away your time.* John liked to sit and read in there. Still does. David was the one who needed help with maths. Peter couldn't spell. He needed rules, like 'i' before 'e' except after 'c', and homespun spelling bees.

I could recite my nine times tables perfectly.

2

Our literacy improved reading Footrot Flats or Joliffe's Outback, torn and tattered rejects from Dad's barbershop. While we laughed at Saltbush Bill's trials and tribulations, they were not our own. I bought comic books with money saved by taking empty coke bottles back to Jacky Bryant's grocery shop—sixpence on returns—stolen from the pub next door.

I gave up petty theft before I was caught and punished with the razor strop.

3

As each of us reached puberty, a special book was handed down like clothing older siblings had outgrown. I'd seen the illustrations scrawled in chalk or charcoal on public toilet walls or on concrete pylons beneath the bridge across the Cudgegong. The book was called, 'The Stork Didn't Bring You'.

I never thought it did.

Division of labour

Both my parents worked fulltime.

At home, outside jobs were divvied up
between three boys. The ones inside
the house were mine—all mine, and Mum's.

We weren't paid to help around the house
but Julie swears I shared four bob with her
one time she helped me clean the bath.

It's not as if I wanted to cut grass
or pass my time in a backyard
woodheap with an axe—

housework made me a time and motion
expert—helped in later life
but I liked trapping rabbits.

They were two and six a pair.

After work Dad took Mum home,
drove to the Soldiers' Club. She cooked
our dinner on a *Metters* fuel stove.

Weekday evenings,
Mum split kindling, cut wood,
kept fires burning.

Pa Nelson

died when I was ten.
He was a quiet man.
Sat in a lounge chair
when he wasn't standing up
beside a barber's chair,
scissors in one hand,
black fine-toothed comb
in the other.

The day he died,
Dad drove to school
to tell me—pick me up,
take me—who knows where?
I don't remember that.
I want to walk, I said.
My father left me to it.

Bullens' Circus was in town.

I always liked a balancing act.

My father's dressing gown

Days after his burial, I ask Mum
if I can have Dad's dressing gown.
In the privacy of my bedroom, I slip
first one arm, then the other, into its
long sleeves. The smell of his sweat

and aftershave—a metaphor for
the sweet and sour way we lived.
I remember his attempts to enclose me
in his 1950s worldview: women were sub-
missive wives, devoted mothers. Daughters
did as they were told, didn't answer back.

I recall my father saying, *No son of mine*
will become a barber, and how we fought
when I turned down an apprenticeship
at *Sharon's Hair Salon*, wanting something
more I couldn't name.

The dressing gown hung limp in my wardrobe
for twenty years. Still too big for me, it lost
its manly smell, went to Vinnies with other cast-offs—
mine, and my daughter's—both of us grown out
of one old century's robes into looser clothes.

First dog

On the lino floor
of a fibro house,
I learnt to crawl,
dragging my nappy
in puppy's piss.

Dad called me *Stinker*,
the dog, *Puddles*.

He ran over Puddles
in the cream Prefect.

Crushed us all.

School reunion

Let's celebrate the fact that, unlike some of our alumni
who did not survive to join us here, we can still recall
first love, perhaps betrayal, other lessons from success
or failure learnt here in these square rooms
full of spotty kids in serge uniforms or on ovals
where fists or sporting heroes knocked us for a six.

Inside the bike shed where the infamous Mrs X
bailed me up and bawled me out for wearing desert
boots instead of school shoes—something Christine, her class
pet, did with impunity—a sense of great injustice raised
its head. Speaking up in my defence, she gave me detention
for insolence. Her comment on my last report—
This D equates to indolence.

Behind the toilet block, cigarette smoke wafted
skywards. Like all my plans of insurrection, it
dispersed. We danced in awkward time to *Beatles* hits.
Even Normie Rowe and J O'K found a weekend following
in me. Re-assembled Monday mornings, I sang
the old school song off key.

The only Latin I could spruik was in the final line:

non tibi sed scholae.

I didn't know exactly what it meant but it was writ large
on my hippocampus and seemed to play over and over
in my head till doomsday. Today, the meaning clear,
the motto needs updating.

Times change ...

Presentations over, dinner consumed, I didn't need
a song sheet to repeat the whole damn anthem
word for word, singing out of sync and still off key.

Still my own woman

(Response to Cait Wait's painting, 'Rustbucket', 2015, for Eth)

Rehabilitated by exercises on a cycle, memories on a page, I have plateaued like the country on which I was born. *You need to be thrown back into your life or you'll regress,* says the nurse in charge.

Compliant for weeks, I'm ready to go: thrown back
into my home—perhaps sixty years of memories will return—
perhaps I'll recall where I've hidden the whiskey ...

thrown back into my social world, that wide pool of friendships
old and new, take 'em or leave 'em, those eddies warm and cool
thrown back into my own left frontal lobe that bled in on itself

making me mute but not mutable, searching for lost words ...
thrown back on my children's concern—all in their forgetting
years themselves—more dangerous than being thrown back

on my own devices. They've hidden the keys to my car ...
At home in my eighty-sixth year, I'm still my own woman.
I'm cashed up, dressed up, my pink lipstick is on straight.

With luck I'll walk upright to my grave. I'm not afraid
of death, but I *am* wary of forgetful children who don't
remember learning their independence from me.

... where I am

Reader to poet

(For Billy Collins)

You wonder why no one looks over your shoulder
when you write in your notebook. You speculate
that your reader is a dark, silent figure; an attentive
ghost who stands or sits in an empty room—
the only sounds—the reader breathing, pages turning.

I would gladly fly to Paris, Bologna, Dublin—
even your home town in the good old U S of A—
if it meant catching a glimpse of you with your
notebook. I would willingly stop to look over your
shoulder, if I could be certain you wouldn't tell me to go to hell.

I would happily buy you a cup of coffee, a Portuguese tart
or dinner if we could talk about poetry; yours in particular
or Emily Dickinson's. You might be interested in Les Murray's
latest collection or the notebook that sits shyly inside my
handbag near the fountain pen, reading glasses, condoms.

After all these years I am sick of this one-sided, anthologised
relationship with you; tired of googling your YouTube readings.
Meet me in the Piano Bar of the Florida Hilton next Saturday.
I'll be wearing the low-cut dress with the carnation in the
cleavage, the fish net stockings, the Jimmy Choo stilettos.

We can pretend to be amazed at the serendipity
of meeting like this, notebooks open.

Trapped

She's trapped in a fast-moving vehicle with the enemy.
She might be driving but the person next to her is in charge,

or thinks she is, delivering a speech on the faults
of the driver—dangerous on many levels.

She's silent, thinking of options: she could swerve
across the highway into oncoming traffic. She could

stop the vehicle and push the passenger out
onto the shoulder or while the car is still moving.

She chooses none of the above. Silent, she drives safely
just above the speed limit. At Pheasant's Nest the enemy

floats a question: *If the plane crashes tomorrow, is this*
the memory you want to have of our last hours together, Mum?

Fibber

(An average of three fibs a day, like meals, keeps us healthy.
We deceive thirty people a week, to 'save their feelings'.
Canberra Times, 14 August 2012)

Thank you for saving my feelings, yet again.
It helps put winter in perspective to know
I'm only one of thirty people you have
lied to in the last seven days. It warms my
heart to know you have only fibbed to me
on average three times a day for as long
as we have known each other.

I'm reassured you're an Average Joe,
not an Honest John. I could never love
an Honest John. If you were moderately
depressed like Honest John, you would,
according to the latest study, tell me
the Awful Truth—the red silk dress I love
so much makes my bum look like
a **(__!__)**

Fibbers are more creative, so the story goes.
They want to save the world from hurt,
whereas the founder of the Radical
Honesty Movement *has no time for the bland-*
ishments of everyday life. He tells his wife
exactly what he thinks; he tells his boss
where he can go; expects both to simply
take it on the chin.

Darling Joe, rub your designer stubble
across my tender breast. You look so cuddly
in your fleecy-lined tracksuit. Your gorgeous
balding head, your morning breath
is such a turn on.

Tying up loose ends

He came when he thought no one would be here
but my daughter came home from school early
to startle him as he emerged from the toilet.

Oh, hello, he said, I'm picking up my orchids to repot them
with a friend. Asking if she would be okay and hearing
she would, he took his orchids and backed up the drive.

This is what I imagine: he bleached the toilet while he was here.
He noticed that I have thrown his toothbrush out.
He saw the dog shampoo on the edge of the bath and cringed.

He checked to see if our photo was still beside the bed.
He read my journal. He patted himself on the back
for extricating himself from a relationship

in which alarms go off in the morning, dogs sleep inside
children have untidy bedrooms and need their mothers.
I didn't imagine he kept the house key.

Questions for a prospective lover

for Laura

Do you take medication?
Are you a sport or gym junkie?
Do you smoke? What's your poison?

Do you love your mother?
Did you and your father get along?
Sibling rivalry: is there some?

Have you been married before?
Are there children involved?
Ages? Do you see them often?

Is the relationship with your ex-wife
civilised or are you in the Family Court?
Are you seeing another woman (or man)?

Questions aside, the acid test will be
if you know as much about me
as I know about you, after this coffee.

Seven meditations on life in five lines and a new millennium

1 One day out from a colonoscopy
the house is constipated;
your plumber can't come.
You go to Bunnings,
buy a plunger.

2 The father of your child visits
for the first time. You follow
the counsellor's advice not to
serve champagne,
sleep with him.

3 Computer and iPhone no longer
compatible. Nothing's streaming,
even though the iCloud has burst.
You book a place
at the Genius Bar.

4 A lover's lies unravel,
one by one. You pick
up the thread, knit
a new reality, stitch
by bloody stitch.

5 Night sweats & mood swings
just as your daughter
hits puberty. You forego
HRT, count to ten;
buy champagne.

6 You need a massage
but the jalopy you call
The Shit Machine
needs a new clutch.
You drink champagne.

7 Time & motion man,
your new boss. You
know it will end in tears
or gaol time—
arrange a secondment.

For love

I have fallen over low fences, climbed
through open windows late at night,
boarded buses, planes and trains, for love.

For love, I have lived in remote villages
in Papua New Guinea and desert settle-
ments where my birthday was forgotten,

several birthdays in succession. For love,
I overlooked these lapses in behaviour.
I have washed double sheets by hand,

eaten stuffed bullock heart and other offal
and complimented the man who dished it up.
For love, I put up with injured plovers

in the bathroom, kept emu chicks in
laundries and cleaned up their mess. I have
placed edibles next to the bodies of glad-

wrapped birds in freezers that my lover
planned to dissect at a more convenient
time for some scientific purpose.

He never did. And there were many days
I held a spanner or a wrench for a man
intent on fixing an engine that wasn't

ticking over, fitting this service into my
busy day of house-keeping, accomplished
without any help from the man concerned.

When he preserved a woman's uterus
in formaldehyde and kept it in a jar,
sat this curio on the dressing table in our

'boudoir', it seemed like an act of sorcery.
Perhaps it represented me somehow ...
In dreams, for I had many, there were gardens,

a child, or simply a life of *my* design; money
of my own. Awake at night beside his sweating
body—its back to me—the pull between

the floating moon, another woman's body part
and mine was, in retrospect, pure alchemy.
And so, for some small liking of myself, I ...

Ruby lipstick

A man I barely know pays me
a compliment as we walk to a poetry
reading near Lake Disappointment.

Surprised, I mumble my thanks.
Apparently, he finds the ruby lipstick
I'm wearing 'exciting'. What it does

for me is lift my pale, ageing spirit
in the morning mirror. He offers
to *break my bones* in nearby bushes.

I could laugh. I could say, *Let me*
consider that tempting offer for a
minute, you silver-tongued devil,

but my hot lips are pressed tight
against the fur ball of embarrassment
rising in my throat. I could take

the moral-high-ground and say, *fuck off,*
throw him the curveball of some feminist
rant or recommend an old-fashioned,

self-improving book like
How to Win Friends and Influence People
but the mothball of recognition—

its stink settled in the hand-knitted
layette of memory—comes to mind
instead. I say nothing.

I sit apart from him in late summer sun.
The words of Berryman, Heaney, Larkin
float past like dead leaves in autumn wind,

Elizabeth Bishop's translation of *The Cemetery*
of Childhood buries us in the 'flesh, ash and earth'
of our inarticulate and ordinary loneliness.

Subtropical postcard

There's something on my mind—
  not today's headlines
  last week's work skirmishes
  or that old dirge
  You did this; I did not
  echoing across the years

Here, now
  all I can think about is
being back on the glass bottomed boat
  sliding into the sea
finned and masked, floating on the rise
  and fall of the swell
watching as our daughter's hair billows around her face
  full of wonder
as she reaches out to touch
  the shell of a green turtle

Water, like art

(After Edgar Degas' Woman Seated on the Edge of a Bath Sponging her Neck, 1880-1895 62.2 x 67.5 cm, Musée d'Orsay, Paris, in an exhibition of his work at the National Gallery of Victoria, Melbourne, 2016)

Even when water was scarce
I have never sat on the edge
of a bath to sponge my neck.

When tank water was low
I stood beside a basin or a bucket
of warm water using a soapy

flannel to wash behind my ears,
under my arms, between my legs,
in that order and as quickly

as possible. But in Paris in the
1880s, women sat on the edge
of a bath sponging their necks

leisurely—or for a lifetime—
their backs to an open door,
the curve of their buttocks,

the arch of their backs, the hint
of breast in shadow captured
in folds of sumptuous colour ...

So French. Today as I stand
inside Degas' bathroom,
behind a woman on the edge

of a bath while she sponges
her neck, I wonder how much
he paid her to pose and whether

she knew her beauty (already
fading) would endure on this
gallery wall, in a southern

hemisphere, well into the 21st
century, when water, like art,
has become a commodity.

Elegy for my mechanic

For Ron

What do you do when your mechanic dies suddenly?

You go to the graveside service, commiserate with his family and friends,
make a donation to Claire Holland House in lieu of flowers,

think about that holiday in Europe he was due to take—his first overseas—
make a mental note to do the next thing on your bucket list while you

still live and breathe. You might recall the time he helped you buy that old
Cortina hatchback—*The Shit Machine*—it was an awful mustard colour,

almost brown, and smelt like mice were nesting in its springs, but it could go ...
or you might remember the way he took *The Beast* off your hands for spares

after you wrote it off running up the backside of that old bloke who braked
unexpectedly on Barry Drive. You might give silent thanks to him for keeping

Trusty on the road, despite the slow oil leak and the coolant disappearing
mysteriously, despite the permanent dashboard light aglow that means

Get Thee to a Toyota Dealer, Urgently ...

You might recall the small talk carried out in cars or in his workshop, the
easy manner of these interactions or how little you know about him, really ...

then you'll ring and book your car in for a service with his son, who's learnt
just about everything there is to know about how things work underneath

a bonnet from his old man, who was only sixty-one and went so quickly, he
left a tread mark on the road as he sped off in his favourite ute, alone.

Florence night

Rodolfo ... I'm alone in your double bed
in this tower overlooking Santo Spirito.
My midnight companions: a full moon,
terracotta rooftops, distant cypress pines.

The condensation on the windowpane
peaks like the misted winter mountains.
This veil on a framed illumination tells me
I'm still breathing, warm-blooded ... a woman

waiting for daylight and you to come
and carry my suitcase down seven flights of stairs
to take the train to Milan where I'll dream
of a tower, your bed, moonlight, Florence

framed by a small attic window
and you ... Rodolfo.

Say Istanbul

After 'Saga of Istanbul' by Bedri Rahni Eyüboğlu (1913-1975)

Say Istanbul and I don't think of crumbling walls
Byzantine relics, Ottoman palaces, churches, mosques
or museums but two old men in a small alcove
under a stairwell who make tea and coffee all day,
a basket raised by rope and pulley taking it
to the morning residents above.

Say Istanbul and I don't think of the Bosphorus
its seagulls, mighty ships or ferries but fishermen
who line Galata Bridge each day and night
their silver mackerel thrown on hotplates
or cooking in pretty barges bobbing on a choppy
current, decks alight, smoke rising.

Say Istanbul and I don't think of Roxelana, wife
of the first Suleyman who, coming from the slave
trade to his palace, successfully implored him
to kill a rival concubine, then his first born son.
I recall good-natured vendors in the Grand Bazaar
spruiking leather, gold, carpets and my blue one.

Say Istanbul and I don't think of going to Gallipoli
but how my father, when alive, had to sit in a certain
chair facing the back door, how he was often angry
but at peace now, buried in the local cemetery, his air
force plaque paid for by a so-called grateful bureaucracy
and how my brother's PTSD manifests post-Vietnam.

Say Istanbul and I don't think of Christianity or Islam
or any take on God or Allah but my mother's maxim
live and let live. I think of citizens caught up in charges
of *insulting Turkishness*, the arbitrary nature of the state—
theirs and ours—and one carved column in the cistern,
its perpetual tears being shed for humanity.

A friend travels to Greece, alone

> *"Joy ... follows rightly confronted despair." Rollo May, 'Freedom and Destiny'*

Grave Circle A at Mycenae—
She's been there several times.
Each time she buries her past
a little deeper. When she climbs
those Early Neolithic inclines,
strolls along their stony paths,
she's far from being a Greek tragedy.
She emails me a photo of herself
with the caption: *My life in ruins.*

She visits the museums in Athens, where
Mycenaean treasures are encased in glass.
One gold sheet, so thin, reminds my friend
of Kylie's hotpants—the ones she wore
in a video clip, which won her the epithet
'Rear of the Year'.

I email back that Kylie's hotpants
are likewise preserved
in a Melbourne Fashion Exhibition.

When she went to Hydra,
I asked my friend to raise a glass
to the dear departed Leonard Cohen,
Marianne—to young love everywhere
and broken hearts. She said she did.

Today she flies to Naxos, famous for abrasives.
She might sip ice and ouzo in the afternoon,
use an emery board to shape her nails,
recall the man who tried to bury her,
and how she excavated what remained,
before she orders dinner.

It will be the sweetest calamari
followed by Sfakianopita.

Manhattan

(Response to Cait Wait's painting 'Under Brooklyn Bridge, NYC, 2015)

The train rumbles through the subway to South Ferry.
The plan is Staten Island, a glimpse of Ms Liberty
and afterwards cocktails, *hors d'oeuvrs* and NY poetry.

It all goes well. Night falls. It's overcast and drizzling lightly.
A honking yellow cab takes me to the famous Bowery.
We cruise past Brooklyn Bridge, Chinatown and Little Italy

until somewhere near the corner of Eldridge & Delancey
he sets me down. I pay the fare and tip him generously.
The gig turns out to be burlesque and stand-up comedy,

which doesn't sound like poetry to me, but I stay.
The stand-up makes me laugh exultantly. It may have been
the cocktails laughing—I had three.

The burlesque is another matter—children's books re-themed;
favourite nursery rhymes dressed up salaciously,
but it's too late to leave—I'm sitting on a fourth martini.

I sip slowly through a *Jack & Jill* a million miles from Disney;
I Love Little Pussy—treated crudely and predictably;
The little lamb that Mary had—feathered, sequined, steamy!

Little Red Riding Hood appears for the grand finale.
First she dispenses with her basket and a little hosiery.
Her silken gloves are thrown, like a bride's bouquet, to me.

Whoosh! She turns, the cape goes west. We see the red bikini
then a twirling wolf's tail circles her behind. She turns. A pastie
covers up each nipple but they're alive and twirl in time!

She stops and bows. All tails hang limply. The audience goes wild.
I slip the silken gloves into my bag, drain my drink, head through
the crowd, casually, whistle up another yellow taxi

while my head goes round, and round, and round, ecstatically.
Oh, New York!! I resolve to have an AFD tomorrow, a change of scene.
Perhaps Harlem's Abyssinian Baptist Church's ministry
where they offer prayers and gospel—another kind of poetry.

An innovator takes charge

A found poem (Financial Review)

A competitive landscape
    artificial intelligence
    blockchain technology
    a brightly coloured nerd nirvana of
    fintech disrupters
    start ups
    giants like Apple

aren't as far apart as you would think
says the surprise hire

loans that go bad
a proctor & gamble
google a chance to dive

    competition one day
    collaboration the next

master the art & the android pays

pipeline, mortar, wriggling, cracks
honcho, butter, factory, banks
disintermediation, breaking ranks ...

massive trouble is the bet I've made

Jobs I would never apply for

Notwithstanding career aspirations and a hefty mortgage
Commercial and Strategy Manager, Transfield Services;
despite the promise of tropical climes, the general *ring* of the title
Executive General Manager, Southern Pacific, Wilson Security;

and because of a personal loathing for the word *compliance*,
its association here with the harsher sounding *branch*,
Assistant Secretary, Immigration Compliance Branch,
Department of Immigration and Border Protection;

and given the documented trauma and abuse, especially
of children; a belief that the buck stops with me
Assistant Secretary, Offshore Operations Branch,
Department of Immigration and Border Protection;

but if there are jobs going in *Transparency Services,*
Benevolent Security or the *Welcome Division,*
Department of Resettlement on Australian Soil
send the position descriptions a s a p please.

Fridge magnets

I exist as I am. That is enough.
Walt Whitman

(it's fading)

Subvert the dominant paradigm
Rainforest Information Centre, Lismore

(Tennant Creek show bag, 1987)

Love conquers war
Sophocles

(I doubt it)

Before you borrow money from a friend, decide which you need more

(teenage daughter's contribution—
she lent me $30 for wine)

How about a nice cup of shut the fuck up?
Anonymous

(puberty & menopause—same house, same time!)

Carpe Diem
Quintus * Horatius * Flactus

(I need to chill)

A career in sustainment

@
Broad
spectrum's
website, jobs with
sustainment in the title
mean you could be involved in
personnel services, the provision
of logistics, administrative purchases
a variety of operational matters or God
Preserve Us 'examining rectums' because
it says you work physically from below. Further
information, found in the Dictionary of Military &
Associated Terms, tells us this involves tasks being clari-
fied & standardised, interoperable procedures being established
& clearly defined command relationships in place that contribute
to
sim
pli
city.
In
other
words
you
will
do
any
thing
and
every
thing
your

imme
diate
boss
tells
you
to
do.
You
will
main
tain
and
prol
ong
oper
a
tions
until
a
success
ful
mission
is
accom
plished.
Con
tracts
are
in
volved.
Sign
here:

....

Saving face (an elegy of sorts)

His burial was a private,
grave-side service. She went
like an Egyptian Queen
        with her trappings:

Ezibuy catalogue
unfinished knitting
sachets of perfume
        hipflask of whiskey

a packed church: the chosen
hymns, the usual psalm, glowing
eulogy, slow drive
        to the pre-paid plot

the wake, held at her Club:
open bar, finger food,
a happy-snap slide show
        spinning tales ...

He's loosely held together
by the woollen cardigan
she knitted for him
        before the rift;

She settles in beside him in her best
blue dress, clipped at the throat
with a marcasite brooch
        his 'I'm sorry' gift.

Inside the dark casket
her mouth, stitched into a smile
for the viewing,
        comes undone ...

Something like a prayer

For John

I thought of you when I woke up
and again when I went through my exercise routine.
While I lifted weights for knotty shoulders
I wondered if you were, at that moment, under the knife
and I sighed, as one does when there is nothing else to do.
During meditation something like a prayer emerged.
There was a brief respite when Jan rang and for the hour
spent at a lunchtime seminar listening to Toni B
talk up the need for Indigenous facilitation and mediation—
still unappreciated and unfunded—nothing much has changed
in that regard except the wicked mess is worse now
everything Indigenous is wedged firmly in P M & C
under Tony's winking eye. I didn't turn my phone back on
until after I'd caught up with Geoffrey. *You've been sick* he said
and I agreed. *Shingles* I elaborated *on my head. You've got a stent, I hear.*
I've got four he said and we shared a rueful laugh. Our small news—
a granddaughter, a breakup in the family, his wife's move
to another job—at last she's left the shitty boss I left some years ago—
my daughter's graduation, the awarding of degrees and medal
by our mate, the Chancellor. What a photo that is sitting on the old piano—
both in academic garb, smiles so large her endearing double chin
made a rare appearance and mirrored mine—the smile, that is,
I have no double chin. Afterwards I thought of you again.
Still no word.
By six I hadn't heard a thing so I rang Therese.
You went into theatre late, you were only just back on the ward.
At least I knew you'd come through—out the other side
of all unspoken fears—alive, alive-o!
I turned the phone to silent once again when Barbara B
picked me up to go to poetry—a nice diversion—
then at half past nine I rang Therese again.

The news was scant but reassuring. Low blood pressure
delayed you in *recovery*. RECOVERY! Now there's a word
I like. You were awake and wanted water
but you cannot have it.
You're on ice tonight.

Afterword

Growing up in country NSW, bush ballad rhythms and images seeped into my green bones like a first sense of home or country. In those days I wrote poems, doggerel, about spats with friends. Then I grew up, stopped that nonsense and left home. After many years in Papua New Guinea, I slid sideways into a job in an Aboriginal settlement in the Northern Territory. In the desert I wrote to work out how to live in a place that challenged me with people I didn't recognise: *my* country, *my* people.

Many of these poems hark back to that time and early practice. Others draw on the busy years when I was parenting and working in Aboriginal and Torres Strait Islander affairs. Poetry was the creative pivot I kept close to my chest over a cuppa for half an hour last thing at night. What energised me, fed the blank page, were the paradoxes, collisions, and differences I encountered at work, as a parent, or remembering my childhood.

Inlandia—named for my inland homes, the people who live there and the rich cultural life that springs from place and character to give me creative juice. For the most part, the poems in this first collection invite you to come with me, not to the vast coastline of Australia or its big cities where most Australians live, but across the Great Divide heading west then north; across time zones—or a life span—with its sharp curves, straight stretches, 360 degree horizons; across cultures. In experiencing other cultures close up, seeing many sides, one might sense or reimagine a different, better whole—self, nation, world.

Significant homes—Aboriginal sovereignty has never been ceded

Mudgee, NSW, Wiradjiri country (1950-1968)
Lajamanu, NT, Gurindji country, Warlpiri people (1981)
Tennant Creek, NT, Waramungu country (1986-1988)
Alice Springs, NT, Central Arrernte country (1989-1995)
Willowra, NT, Lander Warlpiri country (2013-2014)
Canberra, ACT, Ngunawal country (1995-

Notes

p. 9, *balanda*: whitefella; *Mimih, Yawkyawk, Wangara*: spirit beings

p. 10, *gunja*: marijuana; *Rom/Mandayin*: customary law ceremonies

p. 15, Dead end narrative (triptych): Between 1998-2014 Cait Wait repainted *First Time Inside* several times, giving me the idea for a three-part poem ranging over a long time span

p 19, *Troopie:* 4 x 4 Toyota Troop Carrier; *tjuringa*: men's sacred object

p. 25, *gardiya*: whitefella

p 32, *tjanpi:* 'grass' in Pitjantjatjara; *ininti:* 'red bean' from the red bean tree in Pitjantjatjara

p. 40, wooden dance floors can be slow, fast or just right. Pops (sawdust soaked in kerosene, linseed oil etc.) made them just right

P. 54, *Non tibi sed scholae*: not for self, for school

p. 68, *break your bones:* have sex

p. 77, the reference to Kylie's hotpants: http://www.dailymail.co.uk/tvshowbiz/article-3799188/Kylie-Minogue-debuted-gold-hotpants-Spinning-London-fancy-dress-party.html#ixzz4iRxg7ICW

p. 79, pastie: cover for a nipple, worn by dancers or strippers

p. 80, AFD: alcohol free day

Acknowledgments

Many people mentored or encouraged me: Kathy Kituai; Nicola Bowery and Harry Laing; the Strathnairn Poets (Moya Pacey, Sandra Renew, Lesley Lebkowicz, Sue Peachey and Hazel Hall); Owen Bullock and Paul Hetherington in particular. Indulgent friends, who read, listened to or commented on many of the poems include Phil Donnelly, Margy Wylde-Brown, Janet Millar, Helen Maxwell, Sarah Rice, Jo Rendle-Short, Kim Mahood, Sue Fielding, Judith Carswell, Peter Cavanagh, Patrick Markwick-Smith, Alison Laycock, Tim Rowse, Jan Mackay, Ann Port, Jacquie Bethel, Greg McAdam, Cathryn McConaghy and the Warraweena artists. My Mum, Eth, liked everything I wrote. My daughter, Noni, has a fine ear. My brothers like me to keep it down to earth.

Thanks too, to Manning Clark House and Judith Crispin for the first opportunity to read in 2013 and Geoff Page who published my work and gave me opportunities to read at Poetry@Gods and Poetry@House.

To long-time friend, Cait Wait, thanks for working with me on *A Chosen Life*, our joint exhibition/performance at The Residency in Alice Springs in 2015.

The generosity, eye and ear of Owen Bullock for editing the manuscript and Shane Strange for publishing it is greatly appreciated.

Paul Hetherington thought to direct me to Sibelius' *Finlandia*. The beauty, diversity and sheer size of inland Australia imitates the sweep and mood of the music.

To the Lander River Warlpiri, especially the Nampijinpas, and the Directors of Alekarenge Horticulture Pty Ltd, thank you for your continued generosity and humour.

* * *

Several poems in the collection have been previously published in *Overland Literary Journal; Award Winning Australian Writing; Island online*; the 2014 NT Writers Centre Literature Awards booklet; an *Australian Poetry Members Anthology*; the anthology *The House is Not Quiet and The World is Not Calm, Poetry from Canberra*, edited by Kit Kelen and Geoff Page; the Mudgee High School Centenary Magazine; the ACU chapbook, *Peace, Tolerance & Understanding*; *Best Australian Poems 2015*; the ACU chapbook, *Joy; Westerly online: Crossings; Mascara Literary Review*; Newcastle Writers' Centre *Grieve Anthology*; *Not Very Quiet* and *The Canberra Times.*

K A Nelson was born and raised in Mudgee NSW, left school at 15 and went to 'tech' to learn shorthand and typing. A decade or so and a few adventures later, she returned to study with the help of Prime Minister, Gough Whitlam, first at Sydney Teachers College, then at the University of New England. With a Diploma of Teaching (Technical) and a Bachelor of Arts majoring in English literature and Drama, she returned to the desert.

K A Nelson has lived and worked in New Zealand, Papua New Guinea, Italy, the Northern Territory and Canberra. After three decades in Aboriginal and Torres Strait Islander affairs she's back studying at the University of Canberra, writing a memoir with poetry as part of a Masters by Research.

Her greatest achievement and joy has been raising her daughter with lots of love and community development principles.

2018 Editions

The Uncommon Feast **Eileen Chong**
Inlandia **K A Nelson**
Peripheral Vision **Martin Dolan**
Ley Lines and Rustling Cedars **Niloofar Fanaiyan**
The Love of the Sun **Matt Hetherington**
Moving Targets **Jen Webb**
Things I Have Thought to Tell You Since I Saw You Last **Penelope Layland**
The Many Uses of Mint **Ravi Shankar**
Abstractions **Various**

2017 Editions

A Song, the World to Come **Miranda Lello**
Cities: Ten Poets, Ten Cities **Various**
The Bulmer Murder **Paul Munden**
Dew and Broken Glass **Penny Drysdale**
Members Only **Melinda Smith** and **Caren Florance**
the future, un-imagine **Angela Gardner** and **Caren Florance**
Proof **Maggie Shapley**
Black Tulips **Moya Pacey**
Soap **Charlotte Guest**
Isolator **Monica Carroll**
Ikaros **Paul Hetherington**
Work & Play **Owen Bullock**

all titles available from
www.recentworkpress.com

RECENT
WORK
PRESS

www.ingramcontent.com/pod-product-compliance
Lightning Source LLC
Chambersburg PA
CBHW032046290426
44110CB00012B/970
9780648257905